INTRODUCTION TO INSURANCE 101

Beginner's Guide to Life Insurance, Health Insurance, Homeowners Insurance, Car & Auto Insurance, Travel Insurance and Business Insurance

Owen P. Walcher

Ask A Friend Publishing LLC

Ask

Copyright © 2022 Owen P. Walcher & Ask A Friend Publishing

All rights reserved

The characters and events portrayed in this book are fictitious. Any similarity to real persons, living or dead, is coincidental and not intended by the author.

No part of this book may be reproduced, or stored in a retrieval system, or transmitted in any form or by any means, electronic, mechanical, photocopying, recording, or otherwise, without express written permission of the publisher.

ISBN-13: 9798358955240

CONTENTS

Title Page
Copyright
Introduction
Preface
Insurance Overview — 1
Insurance History and Current Trends — 7
Life Insurance — 12
Health Insurance — 16
Homeowners Insurance — 20
Car / Auto Insurance — 27
Travel Insurance — 34
Business Insurance — 39
Epilogue — 45

INTRODUCTION

This book was written as a basic primer on Insurance, so that you can make informed decisions about how best to manage the risks that exist in life.

It should not be construed as legal advice. Proceed at your own peril, just as all other things in life.

PREFACE

For more information, and access to the most Frequently Asked Questions (FAQ) regarding Insurance, visit our website at:
https://www.InsuranceFAQ.me

From there, you can find answers to many questions folks have already asked, submit your own question to the Insurance Gurus, and follow the links to answers presented in video format via our YouTube channel.

◆ ◆ ◆

You can also get online quotes from our website here:
https://www.InsuranceFAQ.me/get-quote

◆ ◆ ◆

Access our YouTube Channel directly here:
https://www.InsuranceFAQ.me/youtube

INSURANCE OVERVIEW

Picture this, disaster strikes, say, a fire, legal action, theft, or an automobile accident. In this case, you will need assistance recovering losses through a financial safety net. The safety net in this scenario is the purpose of Insurance.

What Types of Insurance are There?

There are two classes of Insurance; Individual Insurance and Business Insurance. Some individual types of Insurance that you may or may not already know include;

Automobile Insurance:

The most popular form of Insurance is auto insurance. All states mandate that automobile insurance coverage be at least minimal. The standard auto insurance policy includes liability protection for personal harm and damage to property, costs incurred in treatment, automobile damage to or its loss, and legal expenses regarding litigation.

Life Insurance:

When you pass away, life insurance caters financially to your loved ones, including designated legatees. There are two main types of Insurance: term insurance, which only offers protection for the duration of the policy and only pays out upon the death of the insured; and whole life insurance, which offers both Insurance and savings and permits the insured to make withdrawals before passing away.

Health Insurance:

The expense of hospitalization, medical visits, and prescription medications are all covered by health insurance. Many businesses offer the most practical insurance plans that pay 100% of hospital expenses and 80% of prescription drug and physician services.

Disability Insurance:

If an employee is not able to work due to sickness or an injury, this policy will pay a percentage of the individual's wages (or a predetermined amount) each week or each month. Longer waiting periods before payments are due to result in cheaper premiums: Insurance that starts paying an injured employee after a month may be two times as expensive compared to one that delays payout by six months.

Homeowners Insurance:

Insurance coverage covers losses/damages brought on by specified risks such as fire, theft, and others. Any policy does not typically cover all risks. The homeowner must evaluate his demands by considering the potential dangers in his neighborhood, such as earthquakes, hailstorms, flooding, and other calamities. In cases where a policy on a property does not amount to replacement costs of at least 80%, homeowner's policies limit the amount of coverage that will be provided. The owner must either purchase a rider that automatically compensates for inflation or increase the policy limits yearly if there is inflation. Owners of residential or commercial properties may save by reducing the insured amount of their insurance policies in cases where property values have fallen significantly.

Other Liability Insurance:

A person can be sued in today's litigious society for pretty much anything, even a slip-and-fall on the sidewalk, an irately said short phrase, and a baseball field mishap. Under this policy, the personal liability policy covers all the risks experienced. The coverage here tends to exceed that of house and auto insurance policies. Usually costing around

$250 per year for $1 million in liability, this umbrella insurance is not prohibitively expensive.

Business Insurance:

When it comes to Business insurance, the types vary based on the type of business, and some bear similarities to individual Insurance. They include;

Workers' Compensation:

According to the International Labor Organization (ILO), globally, there are approximately more than 300 million work-related injuries and about 160 million casualties of occupational sicknesses per year. Crazy right? Bearing this statistic in mind, businesses must carry workers' compensation insurance in practically all states. A few individuals can accomplish this through privately insuring themselves, which entails keeping aside money to counter the eventuality. In most cases, smaller companies provide this type of Insurance, which private groups provide, public sources, and other professional groups.

Automobile Insurance:

Similar to individual Insurance, companies that use automobiles are required to keep a bare minimum of auto insurance coverage that covers general liability, bodily injury, and property damage.

Malpractice Insurance:

To prevent litigation by angry patients or clients, professionals like doctors, attorneys, and accountants frequently obtain malpractice insurance. During the previous thirty years, the price of such Insurance has increased for doctors, partly due to more outstanding jury verdicts against doctors who conduct their profession negligently.

Business Interruption Insurance:

When it comes to this type of Insurance, an organization buys a policy that covers any possible loss in the employees' earnings in case there is an interruption in the company's operations. Such cases include; loss of power, shortage in supply materials, or strike among the workers. This coverage depends on the size of the organization and the susceptibility to any financial harm caused by the loss of business assets or any other property owned by the company.

Property Insurance:

If you dream of owning a business, this is for you. As a business owner, you can't afford to leave any aspect of your business exposed. Buildings, inventory, permanent fixtures, or any similar goods vital to the company need reliable coverage. Property insurance, therefore, is vital to you as a business owner.

Liability Insurance:

Companies may encounter a number of risks, which may result in a serious adverse effect on productivity. There is a variety of Insurance, including those for landlords, tenants, and homeowners, landlords, and tenants (blanketing losses incurred on all the buildings); for manufacturers and contractors (blanketing losses incurred on buildings); for a business product (covering liability resulting from warranties on products or injuries caused by products); for contractors (cushioning losses caused by private contractors engaged by the insured); and a host of others (for failure to go by the rules outlined by contracts).

Who needs Insurance, you may be wondering?

Well, if your goal is to minimize monetary uncertainties and avoid unintentional loss, then you must get Insurance. You achieve this by meeting a reliable insurance company, trading your assumption of potential risks, and promising payment of a sizable amount of money to that company. This amount is commonly known as a predefined fee, the Insurance.

There is no specific time or age to get Insurance. You can get it anytime; however, if you own property such as a car or a business, there is no more fantastic time than now.

There are a couple of places where you can buy Insurance, such as;

Directly from the provider, via a broker, or from a fin-tech startup. All three options bear their pros and cons and address a specific demographic. For instance, buying Insurance directly allows you to scan the market on your own time and get what best suits you at your budget.

The biggest downside to these criteria is the time you will spend finding what works best for you. In the case of a broker, you save time and get the best deal based on your specifications and overall peace of mind. There is no downside to buying from a broker since they work for the Insurance.

In some cases, however, you might pay more. The last option to consider is fin-tech. This option provides myriad advantages starting with its easy-to-use feature, diversification of products, cost-effectiveness, data security, etc. In the same way, we are different; our preferences are different. That said, I'll leave that to you to decide.

The most asked question by individuals seeking coverage is, why do I need Insurance? To answer this question, you will need to know that:

- Insurance policies are crucial in helping financial balance loss in families. Such loss happens when a family encounters the untimely death of their breadwinner.
  - Insurance plans can also be helpful when settling medical care, hospitalization or treatment of any illness. The insured's family can also use the policy to settle debts accrued in life by the individual, such as home loans.
  - Insurance coverage is essential to a family in maintaining their living standard in case the insured dies in the future. Will your family maintain their standard of living, or will they succumb to poverty and be the town's laughingstock? I am sure you don't want to imagine that. The insurance company gives a lump-sum payout for bills in case of death or medical emergency.
  - Insurance plans, in most cases,

include investing and savings options. The best plan one can have is essential protection. This plan provides additional support to wealth and monetary savings.

- Insurance can help in securing your home if any unforeseeable catastrophe occurs. Your house insurance policy allows you to acquire reliable coverage for property damage. The policy caters to the cost of rebuilding or repairs. You can also choose to use the money to purchase replacement items.

INSURANCE HISTORY AND CURRENT TRENDS

Insurance has played a crucial role in the empowerment of US citizens. It has transformed the lives of youths, families and company owners.

What is the History of Insurance?

The insurance concept began way back in the third and second millennium BC. Chinese, Babylonian and Indian traders employed the insurance concept in distributing and transferring risks associated with their economic activities. Charles Duhigg says that since the 17th century, insurance agents have been the foremost experts on risk. For instance, between 1750 and 1755, the Codex Hammurabi Law formulated a law that directed that any sea captain, ship charterer or ship manager that would salvage a ship from the utter loss was only required to pay half the value of the boat to the ship owner.

This practice by our forefathers has been resourceful. However, over the years, we have seen improvement that includes the sophistication of insurance systems, inclusivity of insurance policies and a rise of many insurance policy providers. Insurance is dynamic. Risks our forefathers sought Insurance against their loss have been solved over time, paving the way for a different set of risks. For instance, business risks that were not insurable before the covid-19 pandemic are now insurable in the post-Covid era.

The dynamics of insurable change depend on the prevailing political, environmental, societal and technological conditions. Different political tides invited additional insurable risks. For example, the Russian and Ukraine battle has posed potential business risks associated with political violence. Wars can cause detrimental effects on businesses. Think of the world wars and how the business sector suffered a significant blow.

Current Insurance Trends

Technological risks have been on the rise during the Ukraine-Russian war. Following developing news about the war, Russia has resorted to cyber intrusions as revenge mechanisms against Ukraine and NATO states. An increase in cyberattacks is a considerable digital risk that can leave many people devastated or even dead. Due to the digitalization of government and personal products and services, we have become susceptible to cyberattacks and cybersecurity failure. With such risks, businesses might suffer high overhead costs from impaired operational systems.

In light of climate change and action, a lot has changed. Currently, we are facing more climate-related risks, including damaging properties of infrastructure found along the coast due to the rising sea levels. An example is Hurricane Sandy in New York City.

Due to climate changes, agricultural production has dramatically reduced in some parts of the country. A national report on the economic risks of climate change in the United States has shown that the Midwestern and Southern counties will experience more than a 10% reduction in agricultural production for the next two decades.

What Does Insurance Offer?

Insurance offers a protective shield in the event of the occurrence of risks. You have experienced or heard of the myriad benefits of Insurance. You can benefit to an enormous extent from taking Insurance. Firstly, health insurance has been at the forefront of protecting the youths from impending financial crises. Medicaid has helped many disabled children and homeless kids. It has also expanded its coverage for youth aging out of foster care.

Youth in their foster years face health risks from mental health conditions, disabilities and drug abuse. Health insurance coverage have been a lifesaver for many children. However, a significant percentage of the youth do not have health coverage. According to statistics by Urban Institute, 49% of the youth have employer-sponsored Insurance, 10% have Medicaid or other public coverage, and another 10% have non-group health coverage. It thus translates to about 31% of youths being without health coverage. It might seem as though the number is small, but I can promise the impact is enormous, and we can all feel it.

Secondly, property insurance has enabled many to empower themselves and their families by owning businesses and properties such as land, buildings and machinery. Just as Millard Drexler would say that you can't run a business without taking risks, we succeed by daring to dream and pursuing the dream no matter the costs. With this property insurance, you are sure to have a constant flow of income from your businesses, making significant investments and owning assets. That is how to plan and secure your future.

Why Buy Insurance?

Living with no life, health or property insurance is a considerable risk. You are gambling with your life, finances, properties and health. Choose to be a planner and not a 'gambler.' Working with an insurance company, some have been good, and others bad. Today, dwell on the positive experiences where someone has applauded the role of insurance companies in empowering and saving them from deep financial pits. For instance, where there have been business losses, car accidents, and disease outbreaks, Insurance has chipped in and made the situation more bearable. Insurance transforms you so much that you don't realize that you once were in a pit. That's the power of investing in Insurance.

Insurance companies ensure reliability through reinsurance as a strategy to lower risk. Reinsurance is the insurance that insurance firms purchase to safeguard themselves against disproportionate losses resulting from significant exposure. Reinsurance is essential to insurance firms' efforts to maintain their financial stability.

For instance, based on models that indicate minimal likelihood of a storm affecting a geographic area, an insurance company may write excessive amounts of hurricane insurance. If the unthinkable occurred and a hurricane did strike that area, the insurance firm might suffer huge damages. Insurance firms might run out of business every time a natural disaster strikes if reinsurance doesn't take some of the risks off the table.

On the flip side, some folks find it hard to get Insurance. Some of the contributing factors are unemployment and a wrong perception of Insurance. With the increasing digitization of services and goods, many are unemployed. The covid-19 pandemic has also increased unemployment since more workers were retrenched and laid down. Unemployment bars you from enjoying employer-sponsored Insurance and raising income to pay insurance premiums.

You can play a significant role in improving your life through Insurance. You are your own barrier to growth, health and financial security. We should work more to understand how we sometimes contribute to our misery. Just as Manoj Arora says that life insurance is mitigation to the risk of your life, financial freedom is mitigation to the chance of living your life! Choice has always been yours. Today, I challenge you to evaluate your life, health and property. Now, imagine losing one or all of these assets due to ignorance. We would be unwise to hear the nuggets we shared in the many discussions and brush them off. Putting this knowledge into practice will benefit and impact this and other generations.

Insurance Feeds Lifestyle

Insurance could become our lifestyle if we adhere to it as our discipline. With practice comes perfection. We might not be where we want to be today, but we can now choose to be where we will be in the future. Learn to take the initiative. Become a responsible person by making an effort to be financially secure. You can start investing in Insurance with the little that you have. Dwayne "The Rock," Johnson said that success in everything will always come down to focus and effort, and you control both.

Cultivating financial security and freedom through Insurance pays. You can earn returns from your premium payments to the insurers. It is a sure path to financial freedom that most people lack, because of poor decision-making, ignorance, and discipline. Who doesn't want financial freedom? Your money working for you is the ultimate goal of Insurance.

Lastly, learn to educate yourself. There is no limit to what you can understand. Do your due diligence by researching Insurance. Knowledge is vital in taking risks. You will know what you are signing up for in advance. Therefore, you develop a mechanism to cushion yourself from such risks. Being more deliberate with improving yourself gives you the motivation to learn. Knowledge brings transformation, and the latter will contribute to your growth in various spheres of life.

With this knowledge, you are entrusted with the responsibility of drawing more and more people to journey with you in securing your future. Be a good 'ambassador' of Insurance. Create awareness of the importance of health, life and property insurance. In this way, you positively impact other people's lives, which is your power.

Insurance is an integral part of your life and every human life out there. So, as you step out there, and while you pursue that career or dream job, you don't want the 'fear of loss' to be a constraint on your growth.

Insurance won't and will never eliminate loss, but it will reduce the risk to you as an individual and will ultimately save you a fortune.

LIFE INSURANCE

There is nothing that is more important than your life, and your ability to make a living. So, it makes good sense to insure your greatest asset- you! It is a brilliant statement that I concur with because safeguarding your future is your responsibility.

What is Life Insurance?

Life insurance policies have been diversified over time to suit our different goals. Protection policies allow insurers to reimburse upon the insured calamity. It can be death, terminal illness, or disability. The most recent policy adopted in our life insurance industry is term insurance.

Most of us might or have already considered this option. The insurance period is short and is about 10, 20, or 30 years. It makes several choices available, especially after the insurance period elapses. You can choose to decrease the term insurance, convert it to permanent life insurance, or oven renew it. Vast options are available, all tailored to suit our diverse financial needs.

On the other hand, investment policies are a form of saving. You get to pay capital in the form of regular or lump-sum premiums. Then upon the expiry of the insurance period, one is eligible to gain the interest accrued together with the principal amount. The government has provided a tax-deferral basis for life insurance policies, which is quite a steal. Most of us know of whole life insurance, universal life, and varied universal life that fall under this category.

Depending on the customer's preference, there is liberty in choosing between whole life insurance and term life insurance. Total life insurance, on the one hand, guarantees lifelong coverage, cash value, and unwavering premiums. Term insurance comes in handy when settling short-term financial problems and has provided a range for up to 30 years.

Universal Health insurance is a form of life insurance that gathers for the insured's hospital costs, including doctor consultations and medicine. The World Health Organization has partnered with the US government to provide universal health coverage to its citizens. An example is the monthly health deductions through health insurance ID cards. Its value has risen an average of $2405 in 2021 to about $2825 in 2022.

When to Buy Life Insurance?

Age, health history, and gender have been the determinants of life insurance policies. The latest data on insurance rates show that rates for a 70-year-old are 1000% higher than those of a 30-year-old. What does that tell you? Age is a critical factor in determining the rates. The earlier you start paying for the life insurance, the better. In the 20s, you get relatively lower premiums than someone in their 60s. Gender also affects the rates. Interestingly, women and girls have a higher life expectancy than their male counterparts.

Variance in payment of premiums doesn't stop at that. You get to pay different bonuses depending on the life insurance you choose. Term life insurance usually has lower premiums compared to whole life insurance. It is due to the difference in the years that the money accumulated. We have already established that beneficiaries receive reimbursement for the insured's death.

Investing in a life insurance company goes a long way to ensure that the deceased family is financially secure after their demise. It would be so disheartening to go through grief and be in a financial crisis simultaneously, wouldn't it? We can all avoid these by planning ahead of time. For instance, young families are encouraged to have life insurance because minors are left behind upon the death of one or both parents. Another category of people who require life insurance are adults who are co-owners of the property, parents with adult children requiring special needs, and people who need burial benefits.

There is an added advantage to having a life insurance policy outside the interest and compensation. These payouts are entirely free. Funeral services are taken care of in this package as well. The beneficiaries also enjoy returns on savings, especially for whole life insurance. It frees them from the constant struggles of trying to raise living expenses after the death of a loved one. These benefits are available to every one of us.

These are at least five insurance companies you can partner with to realize the said benefits.

- **Haven Life insurance company** is a good service provider in the term life insurance category. Services are on the company's online website. It makes it easy to acquire and manage a life insurance policy in the comfort of your home. The sophisticated systems have contributed immensely to the growth of this company. Their customers receive high coverage limits of up to $3 million from five to thirty years. Access to digital will and fitness apps is guaranteed. Applications don't necessarily require medical exams, which is a plus for individuals who value convenience. On the downside, applications are restricted to people 64 years and below. Also, it doesn't offer any permanent insurance options.
- **Bestow Life insurance company** offers affordable life insurance for individuals between 18 and 60. Coverage limits ranges from $50,000 to $1,500,000. The applications are simple, and you get a quick quote and approval to join the company. Coupled with these is a 30- day trial period before agreeing to the policy guidelines.
- **New York Life Insurance** renders various services, including term, universal, and whole-life policies, which build cash value and interest on invested money. They are pretty expensive and have unclear coverage limits and requirements. For instance, a female aged 35 pays $142.67 monthly for a $1 million coverage in 20 years.
- **North Western Mutual Life Insurance Company** offers

all life insurance options quickly and flexibly. They are not available online, so one has to contact an agent for a quote. The coverage is over $ 1 million.
- **Mass Mutual Life insurance** offers financial stability and a higher payment rating. One is free to convert their time insurance to permanent life insurance. With this kind of advantage, the company's policyholders will reap about $1.85 billion at the end of this year. It should compel us to consider making a step to invest in such companies.

Strive to educate yourself about the different policies available. Educating yourself does pay the best return. Just as Koffi Anan said, Information is power. It is mandatory to understand what life insurance coverage to take, the company to partner with, and their compensation terms. It will empower you to make good decisions for yourself, your family, and any other beneficiary. An informed decision by employing the valuable knowledge you've gained. Also, learn to consult the relevant personnel where the need arises.

HEALTH INSURANCE

What is Health Insurance?

Health Insurance is all about quality life. A quality life is a holistic term taken to mean a life with a healthy balance of the physical, emotional, spiritual, and mental welfare of the individual in question. Your physical well-being is a crucial requirement for a good quality of life. You cultivate and maintain your physical welfare by taking health insurance coverage.

Having health insurance is equivalent to subscribing to a quality life. It is a secret that is preached openly; are you open to receiving the same? Alexis Carell carefully articulated this when she said that *"quality of life is more important than life itself"*.

To empower you to invest in your quality of life and reap your returns later in life, consider health insurance. This article discusses what health insurance is about, who is eligible for it, how we can access this service, and why we need it.

Do we need Health Insurance, and at What Cost?

In the USA, health insurance has become the discussion on national television and other social media platforms. A lot has been said about this subject, and more is yet to be said, especially after this discussion. Recently, an ongoing trend has been doing rounds on social media. Citizens are voicing their issues to the sitting government regarding the efficiency, rates, and necessity of health insurance coverage.

Citizens are complaining of broken healthcare systems that are in the interest of organizations instead of the citizens. In 2021, Johonniuss Chemweno highlighted the disparities that were paralyzing the delivery of health services to the country's citizens. The cost of health care is skyrocketing with time, which is disadvantageous to people and families that cannot raise their hospital bills.

What does Health Insurance Cover?

Health insurance covers the hospital costs if the policyholder becomes sick. It covers all sicknesses provided we have indicated them among the insurable perils. With the outbreak of the covid-19 pandemic, life has shown how unpredictable it can be. You can be whole one minute and fight for your life the next. You can certainly comfortably highlight at least one or two instances where life has shown you its "cruel and unfair" side. In 2020, the number of citizens who enrolled for life insurance coverage tremendously shot up, as health insurance does not pay a death benefit.

However much we might say that better late than never, I tend to think the earlier we start planning for a quality life, the better it is for ourselves and our families. Everyone deserves a quality life. We honestly work too hard not to reward ourselves with the best life. It should be our goal and motivation every time. Looking back, our grandparents did not have the best health insurance policies. Currently, we have super affordable and flexible health insurance policies. What are you waiting for? Seize this opportunity and safeguard your life and your family's.

With the increasing persistence of lifestyle diseases, inherited genetic diseases, and even pandemics that are striking harder and harder by day, we need to reevaluate our life choices and make sound decisions about our health and beloveds. Health insurance providers are going the extra mile to customize our policies according to the prevalent health risks and the indifferent seasons of life.

Dental Insurance covers dental treatment costs for its policyholders. In the USA and other developed countries, this is a well-established cover. Some might sound extra, but I promise you that dental treatment costs can be unbelievably high

Like all other insurance policies, health insurance policies are obtained through a broker, an insurance agent, or direct from the insurance company. Acquisition of health coverage is not a one-time procedure. It will require you to do your research, assess your health insurance needs and make a comparison of different health insurance policies. Choosing your best health insurance company, and assessing your future health insurance needs together with the claims settlement records, will give you constructive guidance on your decision consistent with your preferences.

Every journey begins with just a single step. Getting health insurance coverage can be quick or slow, depending on your chosen path in the acquisition process. 'Enjoying the fruits' has to be the most interesting part of your health insurance journey. Imagine going to your preferred hospital and getting quality and affordable treatment without digging into your pockets for not a single penny! It must be nice! We all deserve this kind of health benefit.

Why Do I need Health Insurance?

The fruits of health coverage are timely and life-saving. Health insurance coverage come in handy in the event of unforeseen health emergencies. Health problems and especially emergencies can be financially draining. Therefore, health insurance prepares for such emergencies and goes further to help you budget in advance. That is what quality life is all about.

Health coverage can give you the autonomy to step into the hospital anytime you deem fit. It covers health check-ups, consultations, and any random hospital visit covered by the insurance policy. With this, you become super intentional with keeping your health in check.

The 'burden of paying for health coverage is not only directly laid upon you but is spread over to your employers and the government. Most employers must channel their employees' monthly earnings to their health insurance accounts. It is a relief to the employee. The amount is deducted from the employee before the money is disbursed to their accounts. It is helpful to ensure that you don't default on paying for your health coverage.

The U.S. government has been at the forefront of ensuring that its citizens enjoy good-quality and affordable health care. One recent and well-known government initiative is Universal Healthcare Coverage (UHC).

Final Thoughts On Health Insurance

We can say about the quality of life, but it remains a theory until you take the initiative. John C. Maxwell says that *"our decisions, not our conditions, determine our quality of life"*. your commitment and responsibility will enable you to realize your desired quality of life.

Everyone needs health coverage. It is never too late for those who don't already have health coverage. You are one decision away from living your quality life free from health and financial constraints. Make a decision today and secure your future and that of your family.

HOMEOWNERS INSURANCE

What is Homeowners Insurance?

Home insurance protects against damages to a person's home and other belongings inside, and against property mishaps.

Who needs Homeowners Insurance?

Homeowners insurance sounds like a luxury to some people, but don't be one of those people. You need to understand that insuring your home is a requirement. Imagine the chaos created in your life if you go home and find your clothes missing or your favorite shoes destroyed. For the protection of such property, there is a need for homeowners insurance.

You may not own a house at this point, but there is something you need to understand. Many landlords out there insist that tenants keep Renters Insurance. It may not sound necessary to you, but it is a vital requirement.

When Do I need Homeowner's or renter's Insurance?

As soon as you get into a contract to purchase a home, it's a good idea to begin looking for homeowners Insurance. It provides you time to get your policy in place before closing on the purchase and enables you to compare quotes from various insurance companies.

You typically have at least a month between the time you sign a contract and the day your new house closes. Is homeowner's Insurance a requirement before closing? At closing, you will generally need evidence that you have paid your homeowners' insurance rates for the first full year.

If your landlord or property management business mandates tenants carry renters' Insurance, you must also purchase it. To reduce the possibility that tenants will sue them for damages to their personal property or liability fees, landlords may require renter's Insurance.

What does Home Insurance Cover?

A home's insurance policy covers four types of occurrences: interior, outside, loss or any damage to personal goods, and injury sustained while on the insured property. After claiming these occurrences, the homeowner pays a deductible, and the insurance company covers the rest, assuming you purchased replacement cost insurance.

Interior and Exterior Damage

The insurance company pays compensation if your home sustains damage from fire, hurricanes, lightning, vandalism, and other insured disasters, allowing you to repair or even fully rebuild your home. Regarding this policy, you need to know that disasters like earthquakes, floods, and poor property are not covered. If you need this protection, consider supplementary riders. If you visit a homeowners insurance company, they will remind you as well that these same rules apply to sheds, garages, and any other structure on the property. For this case, you will need a separate insurance rider.

Home insurance covers belongings like clothing, appliances, and furniture if an insured event damages. An off-premises coverage in a home insurance policy allows you to file a claim for lost property for items like jewels. The majority of insurance providers will only offer a range of 50% to 70% of the Insurance you have on the construction of your home, according to the Insurance Information Institute. For instance, if your residence is insured for $200,000, your goods would be covered up to a maximum of $140,000.

Suppose you have a lot of expensive possessions, such as fine art or antiques, fine jewelry, or designer clothing. In that case, you may wish to pay extra money to list them on an itemized schedule or even purchase a new policy with the company.

Possibility of Personal Liability for Injury or Damage on Goods

If someone sues you, liability insurance will protect you. This provision covers even your dogs. Therefore, if your dog bites Maggy, a neighbor, your insurance will cover her medical costs whether the bite happens at your home or hers. Additionally, you can submit a claim to be reimbursed if your child damages her flower vase. Also, just like if someone had been hurt on your property, you'll be covered if Maggy slips on the broken pieces and sues you for suffering or lost income.

According to the Insurance Information Institute, policies can provide as little as $100,000 in coverage, but experts advise having at least $300,000. By purchasing an umbrella policy, you can receive an additional $1 million or more in coverage for just a few hundred dollars more per year.

Booking a hotel room or home During the Construction or Repair of Your Home

Even though it's unlikely you will have to leave your house temporarily, this will unquestionably be the best Insurance you've ever bought. In the event of a covered loss, your insurance would pay for your rent, hotel lodging, dining out, and other incidentals. At the same time, you wait for your house to be habitable once more.

As you sit comfortably in your hotel room enjoying these privileges, you must do it with moderation because some hotels impose restrictions when booking a suite and ordering room services. Find out what your insurance company allows and settle for that.

Why Do I Need Home Insurance?

There are several valid reasons for needing a homeowners insurance policy.

Protects Mortgage Investment

If you own your house outright, there is no requirement for homeowners' Insurance. But for mortgage lenders to agree to fund your house purchase, you must have home insurance coverage. When a fire, tornado, or lightning destroys your home, it is easy to get repairs protecting the mortgage lender's investment.

Safeguards Your Home Structure

A home insurance policy's principal objective is to safeguard your primary investment. In the event of a natural disaster, such as a hurricane, you would suffer a significant loss if you did not have homeowners' Insurance.

It is best to have full value coverage for your home. But it's also typical to have a range of coverage between 80% and 90%. Homeowners' Insurance typically covers significant, moderate, and complete replacement costs.

Covers the contents of the home

You can choose add-ons to ensure coverage for your interior possessions, including valuable furniture, electronics, and home appliances. Always list all your possessions within your home before purchasing a homeowner's policy. An insurance policy may offer full or partial compensation if covered calamity damage or destroys some of these possessions, like a storm.

Safeguarding against natural disasters.

Natural disasters can cause homeowners to suffer significant losses. Rebuilding a damaged home might drain most of your money and put a severe hole in your wallet. You get protection against loss brought on by covered natural disasters if you get a complete house insurance policy. Such Insurance policy riders often offers reimbursement for catastrophes like landslides, floods, and earthquakes in exchange for a monthly or annual cost.

Protection of Separated Buildings.

Your home is not the only place covered by homeowners' Insurance. It also considers adjacent areas like your shed, deck, garage, and fence. The insurance company covers detached structures by up to 10% of the coverage limit. You can alter your policy if you need more coverage for your home's unattached structures.

Where Do I Buy Home Insurance?

Before you step out into the market to look for home insurance, you should consider your property's total replacement cost, the risks it is most likely to experience, and the monthly insurance premiums you can afford.

Once you've determined the amount of Insurance you'll require, compare rates from a few different insurance providers to determine which offers the best deals. Find a provider that balances reasonable prices, security features, and superior customer support.

Looking at these companies might be a good place to start when hunting for home insurance. The companies will also give you an insight into what to expect when making your purchase.

Lemonade

Lemonade insurance makes it simple to obtain quotations and file claims. This insurance provider solely operates online while employing artificial intelligence to give quick estimates and claim payments. You only need to get to their website, fill out a form, and select the coverage you need.

Hippo

Hippo is a top option for tech-savvy homeowners because it utilizes technology for increased home security and customer service. According to the firm, Hippo enables customers to complete the quote process online, obtain a price in a minute, and receive a policy within five minutes. Hippo also offers you. a discount on smart homes. This cover only applies if you set up and agree to use a free intelligent home monitoring system.

Erie

Erie guarantees replacement costs included in its standard policy. This addition is a robust insurance package for customers. This company ranks in the top five, making it one of the best insurance companies for customer service and claim satisfaction. The company's policy also covers roof damage, unlike many other insurance companies for homeowners.

State Farm

State Farm is one of the biggest insurance providers for homeowners. However, if you are for the idea of obtaining several discounts with your insurance company, then you may want to look somewhere else. State Farm offers few discounts. Multi-policy deals and discounts on security systems are in the policy.

Amica Mutual

Amica Mutual offers the best customer service. Another thing you will find interesting about this company is that the contractor database makes it easier to obtain all the assistance needed. Amica Mutual distinguishes itself for customer service on claims.

Why Do I need Renter's Insurance?

If investing in a house is not a priority, then understanding that renter's Insurance is vital. Renters' Insurance adds endorsements and floaters to strengthen coverage on personal items, just as homeowners' Insurance. Jewelry, gadgets, and other collections, like baseball cards, are some common endorsements and floaters protected by the policy.

As a renter, you are at peace knowing that your property is safe and protected by liability and personal property insurance wherever you go.

How Much Renters Insurance Do I Need?

The amount of renter's insurance coverage you need to buy should match the value of your possessions, as well as any included furniture and/or appliances provided by the landlord.. The other option is to purchase higher Insurance than the value of the items in the house you're renting. If the worst happens and everything on your property is damaged, having this level of coverage will protect you.

However, you can decide to get coverage lower than your possessions if you are ready to take the risk that comes with this decision. Individuals who want to save money on this policy consider it. If this is the path you want to take, please note that the insurance company will provide coverage up to certain limitations in the event of a disaster.

CAR / AUTO INSURANCE

What is Auto Insurance?

If you own a car, you understand the benefits of safeguarding your vehicle. For those planning to hold one sooner or later in life, you need to know why it is important to keep your car safe. Auto insurance offers peace of mind when you get involved in an accident, your vehicle gets vandalized, stolen or suffers damage from a natural disaster.

Individuals make annual or semi-annual payments to a specific insurance company instead of paying for auto accidents out of pocket. The company then pays some or most of the costs related to the vehicle damage.

When you purchase car insurance, you are essentially entering into a contract with the insurance provider, agreeing to pay premiums in return for protection against financial losses resulting from accidents or other damage to the vehicle.

What are the Components of auto insurance?

Car and auto insurance policies are made up of specific components, which each cover a different liability and thus reduce your risk.

Body Injury Coverage

If you, as the policyholder, injure someone else, the injury is covered by your bodily injury liability insurance coverage. When you use someone else's vehicle with their consent, you are also insured, as are any family members specified on the insurance policy.

It's crucial to carry enough liability insurance, since, in a catastrophic accident, you could face a significant financial lawsuit. It is advisable for policyholders to buy additional liability insurance than the minimum amount required by the state. This additional liability safeguards money and other assets like your home.

Own Damage Coverage

Own-damage coverage, a crucial component of comprehensive auto insurance, offers protection against any damage to the covered vehicle. The entirety of the Information on own harm is revealed under this policy section. It would help if you decided whether the incident that damaged your car is covered before you file a claim.

Collision Coverage

Damage to your car from collisions with other vehicles, objects like telephone poles or trees, or flipping over is covered under collision coverage (note that collisions with deer are covered under comprehensive). Additionally, pothole damage is covered.

Typically, collision insurance is sold with a separate deductible. Even if you caused the incident, your collision coverage would pay for repairs to your automobile, less the deductible. If the accident was not your fault, your insurance provider might pursue recovery of charges from the at-fault driver's insurance provider. If they are successful, they will also pay the deductible. If you vehicle is old and not worth much, you might consider waiving collision coverage.

Comprehensive Coverage

With this Insurance, you are compensated for losses due to theft or damage from sources other than collisions with other vehicles or objects. Comprehensive incidents include collisions with birds or deer, fire, falling items, missiles, explosions, earthquakes, windstorms, hail, floods, vandalism, and riots. If your windshield is broken or cracked, it will also be beneficial to have it repaired.

Although some insurers may give the glass element of the policy without cost, you will purchase comprehensive Insurance with a separate deductible.

Uninsured and Under-insured Drivers Coverage

You might get hit by an uninsured driver or a driver whose insurance is insufficient to cover your complete loss. In that case, you will receive reimbursement from the under-insured motorist coverage.

This coverage also provides safety in the case of a hit-and-run accident involving a covered driver or if you get struck by an uninsured or under-insured driver while walking or riding your bicycle.

How to Read an Auto Insurance Quote?

The insurance provider promises to cover your losses per the terms of your policy in exchange for a premium payment. Individually priced policies enable you to tailor the level of coverage to your specific requirements and financial constraints. Policies often have a renewal duration of six or twelve months. When it's time to pay another premium and renew the procedure, an insurer will inform the client.

Nearly all states require car owners to carry bodily injury liability insurance, which covers payments related to injuries or fatalities that you or another driver causes while operating your vehicle, whether or not they demand possessing a minimum amount of auto insurance. Additionally, they could require property damage liability, which pays for harming you or another driver of your automobile caused to another vehicle or piece of property.

The coverage limits (your coverage limit) that the insurer will pay for a covered incident and your out-of-pocket expenses, should you need to make a claim, are all included in insurance quotations.

Why do Different Deductible Amounts Affect Price so Much?

Property, health, and casualty insurance products have insurance deductibles. Deductibles are out-of-pocket expenses funded before the policy takes effect and begins to pay claims.

Deductibles vary depending on the insurer, coverage, and premium amount you pay. The common rule is that you pay lower monthly or annual rates if your policy has a high deductible. This rule applies because you pay various expenses before coverage commences. On the other hand, expect higher premiums with lower deductibles. When this happens, the insurance policy starts paying significantly more quickly.

When policyholders file claims, insurance firms can split costs because you pay deductibles. Companies have two requirements for using deductibles: moral hazard and financial stability.

#1. Deductibles reduce moral hazard risk

The possibility that the insured might not act honestly constitutes a moral hazard. Insurance protects policyholders from financial losses; hence, there is a moral hazard: The insured party can freely behave riskily without worrying about financial challenges.

For instance, drivers with auto insurance might feel compelled to drive carelessly. No deductible means they have no stake in the outcome. Because the policyholder is accountable for some expenses, a deductible lower that risk.

#2 Deductibles to guarantee certain financial stability

By lowering the severity of claims, insurance policies use deductibles to guarantee certain financial stability on the insurer's side. A well-constructed insurance policy offers protection from catastrophic loss. A deductible is a buffer between a minor and genuinely disastrous loss.

Who Needs Car Insurance?

Practically all states require drivers to have auto insurance. However, this is different in some states. Drivers in New Hampshire are not required to get auto insurance. Still, they are required to provide documentation demonstrating their ability to cover the costs of an accident if it is their responsibility.

Because the law demands so, most motorists have auto insurance. However, it does not mean you should only get the bare minimum of protection.

When Should I buy Car Insurance?

Owning a car has long been seen as a sign of independence and limitless opportunity. You nearly feel like you are turning up the music and cruising off into a technicolor horizon. The opening sequence is played. However, car ownership comes with sound advice for all the exciting adventures you intend to go on: great driving comes with big financial responsibility.

If you are asking whether you need car insurance before you purchase your car, then the answer is no. You don't have to buy a cover for you to take your first baby home. Most women refer to cars as babies nowadays. You can buy without Insurance, but I don't think you want to do that.

Most likely, you won't be able to legally drive away with your new acquisition if you don't have Insurance. In some states, the registration process typically starts at the dealership, and most states need confirmation of liability coverage. Even though it's not required, having auto insurance is usually a good idea before purchasing a car.

Where Do I Buy Car Insurance?

Car insurance could be available at the dealership. For instance, the lender may offer to arrange Insurance for you if you finance your automobile at the dealership and are obliged to have collision and comprehensive Insurance. Although it may seem convenient, this is not the greatest strategy to find the lowest cost for auto insurance.

The lender or automobile dealer might only be able to engage with one or a few auto insurance providers. You may research and compare rates from numerous insurers when shopping around beforehand. It will save you time and money instead of getting quotations at the dealership.

As a teenager, you might want the same insurance provider as your parents. You need to understand that your parents may had their insurance with the same provider for many years and are thus offered good driver discounts, but this doesn't necessarily indicate that it is the best option for you.

The best action is to shop around and compare prices from different businesses. I will mention some of the short reviews of the top best insurance companies to work with. They include;

Nationwide

For specific types of drivers and various add-on coverages, Nationwide offers reasonable rates for auto insurance. It is a firm to look into if you're looking for auto insurance because the number of complaints against it for that coverage is relatively low. Nationwide provides drivers who wish to cut their rates based on actual driving with a usage-based insurance scheme and a pay-per-mile option.

Travelers

Overall, Travelers offers reasonable pricing for a variety of drivers. The organization is a wonderful option to consider when comparison shopping because it also offers several optional services that can provide you with superior insurance protection. It receives extremely few complaints from state insurance departments.

State Farm

Consider State Farm due to its highly competitive auto insurance premiums and low complaint rates. It is one of the best companies to work with, especially if you have caused accidents in the recent past. If you are looking for discounts while the company is monitoring you, State Farm is the best place to go. However, if you are looking for new car replacements, I advise you to look elsewhere.

Allstate

Allstate provides a wide range of coverage options, from disappearing deductibles to accident forgiveness. In addition, it has a history of having few vehicle insurance complaints filed with state insurance departments, which helps balance out rates often higher than those of its top rivals.

Erie Insurance

Erie has solid coverage options and receives high marks for handling accident repair claims. These benefits balance Erie's variable auto insurance premiums based on your driving history.

Geico

If you're looking for affordable auto insurance, Geico has very reasonable prices for many drivers. Another incentive to consider Geico is the company's low number of auto insurance complaints.

When comparing auto insurance quotes, you might find many different viewpoints on the company to select and the type of coverage to purchase. One of the best methods to save money is to compare prices from several insurance providers. And it's not a lengthy procedure. Finding the greatest auto insurance prices and the right policy requires a small amount of time.

TRAVEL INSURANCE

Travel insurance covers you when you take a trip, generally out of your country. If you are staying in country, then your regular health insurance covers any accident or sickness, and in this case travel insurance covers the cost of your travel, loss of baggage, etc. If traveling outside your home country, travel insurance covers bot the cots of travel and bag loss, as well as temporary health coverage while in the foreign country. It often covers the cost of hospitals, and sometimes the cost of flying you back to your home country.

People travel to different destinations for different reasons. I know that traveling has become a hobby for most of us, and we enjoy our travels coupled with all of their challenges. Traveling doesn't have to be cumbersome lest it seizes from being a hobby.

We all change locations more often than not. A good fraction of us may have traveled from the USA to foreign countries. for university studies.

Once in a while, we encounter bad travel experiences. Such cases can result from time delays in departure and arrival or even instances where we lose our personal belongings through theft or carelessness. These moments are usually so unattractive because who fancies such inconveniences?

We will first establish what travel insurance entails, who needs this service, why it is essential to secure one, and where we can get such services in different parts of the globe. So, therefore, take up your safety belts and let us travel the travel insurance world! I promise this will be a fun-filled trip with myriad experiences and life lessons.

What is Travel Insurance?

Travel insurance covers claims from people traveling abroad, including their medical expenses, travel delays, loss of personal belongings, and self-inflicted liabilities. International travelers do experience challenges in prepping and doing actual travels. Time delays are prone to happen to any form of travel. International travel delays in departure can be caused by poor time-keeping by either or both the airport staff and the travelers.

Observing time is a precautionary safety measure in international travel. According to the World Health Organization (WHO), travelers ought to seek advice on the potential risks at their travel destination. Doing your research on your destination gives you a glimpse of what to expect concerning your health.

Delaying take-off time is a sure way of delaying the arrival time. Arrival time delays occur due to unforeseen calamities during the travel time. For instance, for air-transport users, sudden unforeseen weather and climate changes during travel may extend the travel time by a significant margin which affects the arrival time.

Mechanical problems with transport vessels, mostly the planes, can significantly affect time travel. I know a good fraction of us have had a firsthand experience with time delays. It is funny how for most people, these delays occur during times when we are in haste. It may not be a coincidence, and perhaps we can look into the 'science' behind that in the future.

Loss of personal belongings during travel has to be the grandest travel nightmare ever. It even gets worse for people traveling to a place for the first time. The culminating effect is that it is not always a guarantee that you will get your belongings back. It can be scary, considering that the lost items are the basics we need to start a life abroad.

Medical expenses vary across borders. For instance, in the U.S., hospital costs are relatively high compared to other countries. Therefore, getting travel health insurance under travel coverage is smart if you want to safeguard your health and finances. Insurance shall come in handy in case of hospitalization, cost of prescribed medicines, and surgical procedures.

Travel insurance is an effective way of safeguarding our belongings, providing a cushion against inconveniences due to time delays, and ensuring our health in case of medical emergencies during travel.

Who should get Travel Insurance?

Everyone is eligible to have travel insurance coverage. However, it is a go-to for everyone looking forward to traveling abroad. With the rising prevalence of covid-19 pandemic and instance, in 2020, most companies in different countries formulated medium expenses cover for their visitors. The number of travel inconveniences almost doubled during this time. However, the coverage provides a good cushion to counter such inconveniences.

For most foreign countries, only visitors staying in the country for a long time are required to have travel insurance. For those planning on visiting for over 90 days and are in the process of applying for a visa, getting travel insurance will be mandatory in the visa application. And more and more countries are requiring you to have travel medical insurance, even for short vacation visits.

Getting travel insurance means signing up for a cost evaluation process. It can be tedious and super engaging for travelers, but it is worth it. During this process, the destination of travel, duration of stay, age of travelers, and medical history are crucial factors the insurance provider considers before issuing the policy.

When to get Travel Insurance?

As a traveler, you are issued the policy before departure from the airport. A thorough assessment of the variety of policies for different companies will be useful in deciding a travel insurance policy that suits you best. Always seek expert advice in such decisions. For this type of Insurance, buy directly from the insurer. With these policies, there are many consultations between the insurer and the insured. Therefore, an in-person discussion with the company's experts will be prudent and rewarding in the long run.

One can never go wrong with getting a travel insurance policy. It ensures that you have a smooth stay in your travel destination and that all that can disturb you are well catered for. What a relief! Living and adjusting to a different country can be challenging. Now imagine this coupled with illnesses, loss of belongings, and unforeseen delays. That can be depressing and make travel boring instead of an exciting adventure.

The medical coverage under travel insurance is resourceful in providing easy access to quality, affordable, and emergency healthcare services. More to that is the medical evacuation advantage. The cover will do the 'work' of transfer from a foreign country to a home country. In extreme cases such as the insured's death, the medical will also facilitate the repatriation of the body to the home country. Who doesn't like such a well-thought medical package?

In some cases, unforeseen personal liabilities and time delays can cause cancellations of flight or ship tickets. A travel insurance policy comes into effect in such cases and covers travel cancellation fees and lost deposits. Therefore, no hope is lost in cancellation since travel insurance policies will offset the process dues.

Offering alternative transport means during long delays is one of the thoughtful benefits of travel insurance. You don't necessarily need to cancel your travel because of delays.

Also, your luggage is well taken care of. In case of theft, loss, or damage of personal belongings, the travel insurance policy comes in handy.

Indeed, travel policy is the "jack of all trades" regarding international travel. It has all the travel essentials you will require to adjust comfortably to a new environment. It is making international a lot easier and more convenient.

In the current travel market, travel companies have provided their clients with travel coverage, such as Travel Angel Life Insurance. They act as middlemen between the insured and the insurance company.

Planning for your travel is planning to have a good time in your travel destination. Unplanned travels can be chaotic and financially draining; therefore, embrace Insurance to plan your dream future.

BUSINESS INSURANCE

Catastrophes can crop up in your family, business, and any area of your life.

Situations like sudden death, business failure, medical emergency, and property damage, among others, can steal your peace, and with a lack of this peace, there is no productivity. Bearing the financial impact of such circumstances can burn a hole in your pockets. You may be forced to dip into the family savings or hard-earned money. And this is where Insurance comes in.

What is Business Insurance?

You can't rush to get business insurance coverage without understanding the meaning of the business insurance itself. Businesses are protected from financial challenges by business insurance coverage that includes accidents that could happen on the job. The business environment comprises different departments, including employees and business properties.

There is various Insurance available for businesses that cover all the aspects of the enterprise. It includes protection against employee injury, property damage, and legal responsibility. Based on prospective risks, which change with the business environment, businesses need to evaluate their needs to obtain the best insurance policy.

What to do Before Obtaining a Coverage?

Small businesses are not exposed to financial loss when compared to developed companies. However, this does not mean they differ from large businesses in obtaining insurance coverage. Business owners should pay extra attention to and evaluation of their business insurance needs. You should consult with a trustworthy, knowledgeable, and professional insurance broker if you don't feel you can accurately assess the risk involved and the need for insurance coverage. You can consult your state's insurance body to get a list of authorized and reliable agents.

Business Insurance Types

There are several business insurances options for small business owners to think about, such as the following:

Insurance for Professional Liability

Professional liability insurance protects against negligence lawsuits brought about by errors or poor performance. There isn't a professional liability insurance policy that fits everyone. Every industry has particular issues that need to be handled.

Real Estate Insurance

In the event of a storm, fire, or theft, property insurance covers the inventory, equipment, signage, and furniture. Mass-destruction incidents like earthquakes and floods are not covered. You might think of getting a different policy if you intend to open a business in a location that is vulnerable to these issues.

Personal property with a significant value is also an exemption; it is protected by purchasing a "rider" to the policy. When claiming the Insurance, the coverage pays to replace costs caused by the damage or give the actual worth of the damage caused.

Liability Insurance for Products

Product liability insurance is crucial if your company produces goods for sale. Any business can get named in a lawsuit for harm caused by products. Product liability insurance can save your company from such a situation.

Automobile Insurance

Any car utilized for business purposes needs to have complete Insurance. Businesses should, at the very least, carry third-party liability insurance, but comprehensive auto insurance also protects the vehicle in the event of an accident. Employees' Insurance protects them in the event of an accident if they use their vehicles while working for the company. One significant exception is when someone, such as delivery employees, provides goods or services in exchange for payment.

Insurance Against Business Interruptions

Businesses that need a physical place to conduct business, such as retail outlets or manufacturing facilities, are well suited for business interruption (or continuation) policies. When an event disrupts the regular flow of business, business interruption insurance reimburses the company for its lost income.

Home-Based Enterprises

Individuals run businesses from the business premises. However, you will find several people who choose to run businesses from their homes. You might be thinking that this is the best idea for your venture, but there is something you should know before you take that path. Like commercial property insurance protects businesses, homeowner's policies do not offer the policy to home-based businesses. Therefore, it would help if you asked about additional coverage for inventory and equipment if you run a home-based business.

Business Continuity

Insurance is essential for your business, but it is not enough to ensure continuity in your company. I want to talk briefly about the business continuity program. Since Insurance against loss is frequently insufficient, there is a need to stress on Business Continuity Program.

Why Business Continuity?

Isn't a company's continued success the goal of everything it does and every investment it makes? It is a question people intending to venture into business have. There are several reasons why you need a business continuity program.

- A good business continuity plan encourages the prompt making of appropriate decisions. Making poor or uninformed decisions in the initial hours or days after a disaster can be expensive. Business continuity planning offers consistent customer service at a minimally acceptable standard. It also ensures that essential operations continue to run during a crisis. Each of these objectives has a large financial effect. If they are incorrect, additional financial loss will result.
- Planning for business continuity addresses issues that commercial Insurance does not. Most business insurance policies only cover loss or damage to your inventory and equipment. Usually, they don't compensate for lost profits. The insured must provide proof of the company's most recent net income to obtain business interruption coverage. The coverage, normally restricted at $30,000 per incident, may be far less than what the insurer needs to continue operations. In some circumstances, having a business continuity plan in place may require better terms from the insurer.
- Planning for business continuity improves your competitive advantage. A tried-and-true method for company continuity offers a considerable competitive edge. It demonstrates to future and current clients that you are a reliable supplier or service provider in their continuity planning. If you desire someone's business, you must have a strategy for keeping them as customers.
- Planning for business continuity results in a deeper comprehension of the company, what it does, and what is most crucial. The business impact analysis is a crucial planning tool for any business continuity strategy. Examining the inter-dependencies between each organizational component is a step in the process. However, following a disaster, some elements are more

important than others and require more time and resources to be addressed.
- Regardless of size, business continuity planning is crucial to any organization's governance and survival ability. No business, whether regulated or not, large or small, should operate without a business continuity plan. Smaller companies are more susceptible to failure after a tragedy. Large firms must show their customers, auditors, auditors, and regulators that they are committed to good governance and can resume normal operations swiftly.

When a disaster or emergency strikes, a well-designed insurance policy will assist in reducing some of the financial damage, but you cannot count on it to fully protect you. These include harm to your organization's reputation or long-term losses brought on by its failure to bounce back quickly or work efficiently. Customers and merchants aren't as understanding as you may believe in today's "me first" society. Customers will question your company's lack of readiness. For this reason, you will need to work with Insurance and a business continuity plan.

EPILOGUE

For more information, and access to the most Frequently Asked Questions (FAQ) regarding Insurance, visit our website at:
https://www.InsuranceFAQ.me

From there, you can find answers to many questions folks have already asked, submit your own question to the Insurance Gurus, and follow the links to answers presented in video format via our YouTube channel.

◆ ◆ ◆

You can also get online quotes from our website here:
https://www.InsuranceFAQ.me/get-quote

◆ ◆ ◆

Access our YouTube Channel directly here:
https://www.InsuranceFAQ.me/youtube

Made in the USA
Columbia, SC
18 October 2023